I Am Not Here To Please The World   Cathy BLUE

Original Name: I Am Not Here To Please The World
Original Language: English

Copyright © Tülay ASLAN. 2021

First edition, July 2021

Book design by Tülay ASLAN
Cover Photo by Tülay ASLAN

ISBN 978-625-00-0215-5

Published by Tülay ASLAN

AF410776

1

I had been thinking of the century we live in, with all these innovations, technologies we have, women are still treated as second class. Educating men has not been solving the issue if you read the rape, violence news, help cries of women from all around the world on social media platforms.

There have been too many things the society chose to ignore, it will be safe to say that they are still turning blind, deaf and mute…

It most of the time comes down to women empowering women. Why do you think? Because all of us had been touched without consent here and there, mansplained, ignored, belittled to keep the fragile men ego intact.

As a woman, I am proud to scream on top of my lungs: I AM NOT HERE TO PLEASE THE WORLD! Sisters, friends, daughters, mothers….Women! Unite!

Together, we will take down the man's world!

Love,

Cathy

INDEX

I Am Not Here To Please The World

I had my ups and down,
Rollercoaster of life,
Do not judge,
We all take our turns,
Life rides us all.

I held my chin up always,
Never backed down from a challenge,
Lost a few fights, licked my wounds,
Came back stronger than before,

I Am Not Here To Please The World   Cathy BLUE

With slier tactics to win.

This world, it is not strong
To bring me down.
I refuse to be tied down,
Submerged into another dull pawn.

Until my last breath,
To my kids and to everyone
Who has the heart to listen,
I will say:
Burn those bridges down,
Do not be afraid to light up the dark!
This world will not bring us down!
We are not here to please the world!
We are not responsible for their fragile egos!
They should indeed be very afraid!

I AM NOT HERE TO PLEASE THE WORLD!

A Mother's Love

Lower me to the ground,
The earth will cradle me
To her chest,
Keep me safe and warm.

Tried to fight my demons
Every day in a million battles,
For once I will find peace
In being a loser.

The earth will shield me
From all of you,
All of this nonsense.
She will sing lullabies,
Rock me to sleep,
Until I rise back up
From my ashes.

Society Versus Me

 They tried to tame her
As if she was a wild stallion.
She was a force to be reckoned with,
A great ally to lift them up.
They pointed their bony fingers at her
Then cried,
She became a sly, restless enemy.

Mating Dance

The monsters under my bed
Wait for the night
To mate with my demons.
They all blossom in moonlight
A never ending conversation
Inside my head.

The Farmer

A black sheep they called me,
"I'll prefer feral seed," I said,
You do not get an apple tree,
When you plant rage and hate.

My Beauty Marks

Never tried to hide or cover
My beautiful scars.
I talk with them at night,
Thank them for their bravery
To take the hit
So we all stayed alive.

Boogeyman Tales

The fear of loss is a path to the dark side,
To be free from all their judgemental expectations,
They had created to keep you in a specific level,
So you do not rise above any of them.

Hysteria

I try to stand under the burnt orange skies,
But I am doubled up in hysterics.
That dumbfounded look on their face,
The look of disbelief then the panic settling,
Their mouths opening and closing like a fish in my net.
If I can not pass that bridge,
Then nobody else can!
Let's burn this bridge down!

Twisted In The Head

The bile rose up to my mouth,
Years of anger, wrath, pent-up frustration,
I smiled down at you,
Pressed a pillow to your face,
Oh baby boy,
It hid behind the silent scream.

I had never been so aroused.

Queen

I am gonna tear up the map
That takes me nowhere.
All it took me was hell,
I danced and played with the demons,
They gave me a crown,
Scorched me goodbye,
Sent me back on my merry way.

Now, now, now,
Remind me again,
Where were we???

Billionaire

I would be a billionaire
If I had thrown a coin in a cookie jar
Every time,
Society dared me to try.

Oh well,
It is so high up here,
I can not see or hear you!

Dance Of A Warrior

I'm gonna raise hell,
You can't keep in me a cell.
The fear in your eyes do tell,
You have never seen a restless rebel.

Hard and unbreakable is my shell,
Your fear, oh, I can smell,
You are all under my spell,
You, I will compel.

In fear, you yell,
Logic and mind dispel,
Your jiggly legs repel,
I've never seen you so unwell.

You are like a dead gazelle,
My spell will always quelle.
The lights in your eyes, pastel.

Ancestors

Beneath the trees, we found blissful sanctum,
Your lips on mine, my legs around your hips,
The moonlight bathing us.
I want to stop but the ancestor speak,
"For every demand you make,
We take and take."

Their screams are too loud,
My vision is all red,
By them, my arms are lead,
I stab and stab,
Your dead body I grab.

They laugh, looking down at me,
They do not understand
What they see.

I may be covered in blood,
But I am not satisfied,
Your blood makes a crimson flood,
With your death, I am gratified.

Bedtime Stories

The cruelty of the gods and goddess,
Good people die too quick,
Evils root in the world.
The most twisted story
I have ever seen.

Revenge Thirsty

Tears of rage burn in my eyes,
''Not yet,''
Whispers the wind,
''Shhh, time will come,''
Wiping away my tears.

Self-Love

Shielding myself
From their judgemental glares and words,
Embracing the power within,
I love loving myself.

Kiss Of Snow

You call me frigid,baby,
I am a snow queen,
I give you a kiss
On your forehead
And many frozen memories,
'Cos your heart has always been
Too selfish and cold to love.

Queendom

All the things you taught me
Made me stronger.
Kill or die,
Welcome to my queendom.

Everest

You look down to me and say,
"It is okay, you are just...
You know, you..."
The silence stretches thin in-between us.
"It is okay to be me," I agree,
"I climbed up this top
With bare nails and many scars,
You only tried to throw mud when alone,
Hold an applauding show when not alone.
And now look, how high I climbed
Once I dropped the deadweight."

Ventriloquist

My heart somersaults,
Full-in, full-out!
"Wow, the execution is breathtaking,
The sequence is so unique."
Yet, Olympic gold goes to a faker,
Claiming she goes higher.
I keep my heart,
He leaves the podium with a ventriloquist.

Poet

"You are wrecked in the head,
Your thoughts are so twisted."
They said in disgust.
I shrugged,
"Hypocrites you are,
You see and turn away.
I am a poet,
I write it down
For many more generations
To read and learn,
The ignorance of humanity."

Aiming The Universe

They told me to aim
For the stars,
If you want bigger, the moon.
I aimed the whole universe,
Can't stop now
Until I reach
What I dream.

Anti-Social

They question why I do not
Prefer to spend my time with them,
"How can being caged inside 4 walls
Can make you happy?", they wonder.
"I walked the bridge of tears,
Left behind my fears,
I climbed up these stairs,
Will not be a pawn of theirs."

Last wish

Set my corpse on fire,
My last dance with fire,
I wanna burn some uncrossed bridges
Before disappearing into ashes.

Blind

Beauty is in the eyes,
Their eyes are blind,
They will never see your shine.

Ash

My devils sing,
I dance
On the ashes
Of our love.

It scorches
My feet,
Ripping the skin out,
I have never felt
So free,
So strong.

Forgiveness

I forgive myself
For all the mistakes
I had made towards myself
Whilst trying to find my way.
I forgive and smile,
I love the woman
I had become.
Was born with a human heart,
Traded it with dragons.

Pain

I scream, *"It bloody hurts,*
Do something, give me some morphine,"
Clutching my rib cage frantically.
They look down and calmly say,
"It is just a phantom pain."

Calls From My Throne

One by one,
I slayed these toxic ties,
Set myself free
From their daily lies.
I rise, never compromise.

Dancing The Line Of Love/Hate

You left, taking away
Every ounce of love that I fought to have.
Selfish and shallow, you would never care,
You had your share,
Again you never see what is rare.
I have always been bare,
With this, a war I will declare.

Retail

I will always taste bittersweet,
You can either suck it up
Or stick with cotton candy ones.
Manager does not accept customer complaints.

Green

I had some good friends in life
Who turned green in envy,
On what I had achieved.

Dull

They will always label your uniqueness
As the weird one,
Be proud not to be a dull clone.

Leap Of Faith

"Faith is everything," you say,
Along with all the other lies,
Trying to push me down a cliff.
I smile, hug you tightly, take the leap of faith.
I open my fiery wings and fly,
Watching the vultures rush to your corpse
In utter excitement.

Skimpy

You line sticky honey kisses all over my skin,
I wanna wash them away.
You hand me paper wings, expecting me to fly high to
the sky,
I wanna tear them away, then burn down to nothingness.
You try to keep me contained in a glass garden of yours,
I stand there with a hammer in my hand,
Raining shards of broken glass
All over your pathetic, skimpy world.

Golden Scars

-Emily, Let's embrace the Goddess
within-

I labeled all the emotions in the jars,
Added my fancy art, over it, tiny stars,
My human body, my Goddess scars,
I tended them with all the superstars.
Oh baby, healing, I feel like a czars.

Tidying The Pieces Of My Broken Heart

Being with you was my burn out,
Like a dagger that i stab myself within
As deep as my heart goes,
Opening my arms wide for the new wave of pain,
Dancing on the ashes of the burnt-out pain.

The last chapter of our story,
Hellfire comes disguised as sunsets.
That shivering silence, those forests of wicked thoughts,
Nothing holds me back,
To paint pain with razor strokes.

Cardboard boxes of traumas,
How long have I been hoarding?????
The splinters of our broken hearts,
They are in too deep.

Love had been lottery tickets,
Few are the winners,
Most are losers.

I am too numb to cry,
I only hum a happy melody
Wiping my blood off the bathroom tiles.

Accolade

Kneel down,
I am gonna bless you
Like a knight,
Forgiving you and myself
For a quick pleasure ride.
I will honor your weapon of choice,
Fasten it around your neck.
Before your head rolls on the floor,
Darlin, you won't even see the blow comin'.

Variety

"Variety is not always good," I explain,
Trying my best not to lose my temper,
-My Goodness, sometimes why bother???-
"Your favourite restaurant has probably
Around 40 dishes listed in the menu,
Yet, you eat the same thing always,"
I try to bring the discussion lower
To your intelligence.
With a smirk you say,
"You kinda described marriage,
All you can do is read the menu
Then eat what is at home,"
You laugh at your own joke.
I smile as well, devilish,
Count the four seasons baby,
After that look at all these menus
And starve at an empty home.

Fair Warning

Oh baby,
I am the alive version of an epiphany,
Smart, witty, creative, strong.
You trying to belittle me
Only makes me laugh at the irony.
I
Was
The
One
Who
Looked
D
O
W
N
At you.

They all knew,
Laughed behind your back as well.

Relationship Goals

Under the heavy pressure of your constant yelling,
My brain shatters into million of pieces,
Mosaic memories of ours
All over the ground.
You have to clean up
The mess.

Sailor

I had always been too much
To handle for a newbie sailor like you,
So many rookie mistakes you did
Being unaware led to the cockiness, these horse glasses.
Lover, even that cruel sea don't define me,
You should have known,
I can not be contained.
You might wanna tuck those sails back now.

Eternal Promise

There is one thing I will promise
To give to you when I leave.
So many haunted nights for you,
Sitting on the coach with your head
Tucked between your hands,
Wondering how and when and where
It all went so wrong.

Moving Out

Your vain heart had always been
A haunted dilapidated mansion for my love,
You claimed it was big enough for both of us,
Your ego could not fit in, I knew from the start.

L(ICE) Cream

''Easy peasy like riding a bicycle,
It would be,'' you claimed,
Topping lies over lies,
Passing me an ice cream cone.

Crimson

I was asked by a medium,
Why my aura looked like
Bleeding all over my body.
I smiled for her truth-seeing,
''All the Phoenix you will meet,
Have crimson soul,
For we burn and burn until
Nothing is left of us
So we are reborn again.''

Freedom

After an episode of steamy work-out,
I lay in bed.
I dream of my freedom,
A caged bird.

PUMA

''Crazy, bossy, restless, ambitious…''
All the other fun names they tried to give me.
I was not birthed to stay where I am,
I was birthed to rise all above you,
Narrow-minded, hypocrite, judgemental onlookers.
You do not climb up the top
Without taking risks
And dropping the deadweight.
Now, read that again.
Slower this time.

Sarcasm Drips Like Honey From My Pen

You, the epitome of humankind,
Always the throw-the-mud-on-someone else kind,
Scream out, dramatize, point your finger to your
scapegoat,
The louder so may be onlookers will believe,
They see it all and only feel sad for you.
God created you without any mistakes, epitome of
mankind.

FireMania

This road I take,
Ups-downs,
Rights-wrongs,
All alone.
You watch,
Hoping for a chance
To stuff me back to the rusty cage.
I will burn more than bridges,
Till the stars,
All burn away.

Birth Of Phoenix

My own personal hell
Comes, wearing a wicked smile
On her perfect face.
Her red, curly hair
Covers some of her
Alabaster skin,
''Come darling,
I will keep you warm and very pleased,''
She coos to me
Her voice deep and husky in lust.
I am eager when I reach for her hand
Chest to chest we stand,
Lips pressed together,
She breathes out, I breathe her in,
Hands roaming on each other's bodies,
She smiles to my lips,
Lacing her fingers through mine,
Wicked she is,
I had never ached so much for someone.
She welcomes me inside her molten lava,
I love it when she burns me down to the ashes,
She comes inside in me,
Whenever I rise from my own ashes.

Life

Gotta make the best of what has been dealt,
It is not like they have a refund or something.

Saving Grace

I will always say *''Nothing, I'm okay,''*
Rather than trying to waste my time and breathe
To try to knock some common sense and humanity
To the shallow minds, deaf and blind.

From A Girl To Another:

But l hear you,
Every man cheers for a strong woman
Until they get one.
Then comes down
The fragile ego
Crumbling down,
Belittling session begins.
OOOOOWWWWWW

What Time Is It?

My mind exploded that night,
Time stopped by, to join my game
Of *how much more can I actually drink?*
The *tick tock* ruffled all my feathers,
Threw the clock to the wall.
Wiping the shards of time from my eyes,
I cry out the time now.

A Cold Dinner

I am standing in front of the abyss,
My feet are firmly planted on the earth,
The wind brushes my hair away from my face,
The ocean sits still beneath me, soft cushion for my fall.
I am waiting for my last sign,
There is only one bridge left,
I am gonna burn it down when the time comes,
My devils are too eager and the pleasure is all mine,
To watch you fall back to hell.
I
Am
Gonna
Watch
You
F
A
L
L.

Finger Painting

One by one,
I cut open all my wounds
I want to heal them
First, I have to take the poison out.

I sit down and watch
The poison bleeding out,
It reminds me of Bob Ross
When he painted in a gray tone only
For an audience who could only see gray.

A little burnt tree here,
A fire lake there,
A little dry grass under,
A faceless sneaky demon on the grass.

My fingers move on their own,
I am trapped and lost
In the long corridors of my mind.
I watch and think,
Wow, Red looks really good
On our white tiles.

BullShit

''Are you lost, baby girl?'' Mimicking a throaty voice.
"Not all those who wander are lost," comes my witty answer.
''OOOOhhhh sassy, I like you already'' thinking you are funny.
"I wish I can ; but I don't want to, play, you are just beginner level!!''

Period Diaries

Bloody hell period of mine
Comes and leaves whenever
Wherever it wants
Without giving a f***,
Whether I am ready or not.

Many times I caught of guard,
Everyone knows I hate
Unexpected visitors
To my own home,
Who gives you the right
To come without a permission after all?
Am I a running a hotel
You can check in and out as you please?

See that anger? This is the tip of iceberg,
Weird but I prefer to be pregnant rather than period,
These stupid hormones, this anger, these cramps,
I double down and howl,
I may need a strong painkiller...

Embrace Of Phoenix

''Hold me,'' I said, all I wanted was
To get into the safety of a hug
At least for a few minutes.
You always got the wrong idea
About what I needed,
Mind always in the gutter.
I burnt myself, along with you,
I rose from my our ashes,
Watching and laughing at the absurdity
Of your skeleton
Finally giving me a hug.

''Burn baby, burn,''
Famous last words.

Driving To The Restaurant

I had sucked most of your bullshit,
Chose to ignore, chose to be a bigger person.
Do you know when was
The start of the end?
The day you mocked my writing,
You buried yourself
Deep pile of my words.

Do tell, now,
Who's laughing now?

F

Fuck you,
Fuck anyone,
Who tries to
Lower my value.

Mud Over The Sun

I chase honesty and sincerity
When you apologize and try to fix your mistakes.
But you roar your cold apology to my face,
Trying to tower over me like a bear,
Guess what baby?
Your time is running out.

Adding Fuel

The automat of your apology,
Rolling from your mouth
Without any remorse or insincerity,
The cold and fed up voice accompanied,
The start of the end,
In repeat mode inside the back of my mind.
I will never ever forget that,
I took a scar, scarred for a lifetime.

Authority

This world is too cruel, too fake,
Onlookers are like fancy judges of a cheap TV contest.
I never fitted in, went into a diet,
Cut these toxic deadweight down,
Added more sarcasm and irony to
My lovely personal traits.
I stood tall and smiled at them, daring them.
Most labeled me as black sheep, b/witch,
But did they leave me alone?

Yes, baby, yes,
Who has won the end game now?

Drinks Are Served

Man, man, man,
Your ego will be your downfall.
I will serve you the poison from my veins,
Freshly harvested,
Sit back and watch you
Guzzling it down in the thirst
Of your self-guilt.

Elephant

If I was to be an animal in your kingdom,
I would be an elephant.
I have the memory of an elephant,
Hatred you name it, I will auto-correct
As *you do not fool me anymore,*
Man oh man,
I can soooooo crush you
Under my giant feet.

Ego Slayer

My words are more resilient than
Your fragile ego.
I'll take the hit, wrap my wounds, and survive.
Who will cower and cry
To the destruction of their fragile ego?

Heavy Sarcasm Of Mine

Me and my brain
Two best buddies,
We pick up on the heart,
'Cos she is weak and cries a lot.

Me and my brain,
Strong boys we are,
Better together
Without a burden to carry.

Beast In The Shadows

Every single day,
Over things that did not even really matter,
You kept watering me
With the poison of your cold words.
I sat down and watched,
''How amazing is that gonna turn out?''
I asked myself.
Now my time comes,
Poison seeps under my skin,
This cold steel is now armor.
You can not penetrate my armor.
No, now you shut up and watch,
How I grow into a beast,
When all my broken pieces bloomed.

Shame Of Cone

Can't stop the itching.
My own skin I am ripping out
Getting high on my own blood,
The more it spills and stains my sheet,
The sweeter release it brings.
Maybe I should wear
A shame of cone,
Like an itchy dog I am now.

Trademark

She wears her madness
Like a dark red lipstick.
If anything,
It only adds more to her charm.

Truths, Just Truths

Behind every strong woman's dazzling metanoia,
Stands a narcissistic, manipulative coward of a man,
Claiming she is a nutjob
Only because he can not control.

Victim Blaming Culture

They had stolen my words, cut my tongue,
They ripped me open, threw to the vultures to feast on.
I tried to scream, I wanted to scream, these tears, this
fear,
They had stolen my words, cut my tongue...

Onlookers, Hola!

Eyes,
Staring back
At my eyes,
Judging all my life,
Useless.

Warrior's Prayer

I wipe the blood off of my face,
Its rusty scent lingers in the air
I breathe in.
I am restless for the next challenge,
I wanna spill more blood,
From head to toe,
Kill and slay all these judgemental onlookers,
For the place they consume,
The time they waste,
The joy they try to steal.

I rest my hand on my sword,
Waving in the air like a salute
Or a quick gratitude to the wind
At my back.

Mutual Feast

I bathed in the essence of you,
From head to toe,
Every inch of my skin,
Covered in your blood.

We had our mutual feast
On each other,
All night long.
We slept, spent and bloating.

Waking up, all hungry,
For another round of my own feasting,
I was like a King on the dining table,
While your blood was my rivers of joy.
I took what you offered, had my fill,
Left the table.

Wolfbane

Was your love a mere stroke of luck
Or a lesson that I was meant to learn?.
All the lies that poured from your lips,
All the useless manipulation tricks,
These small treats of love crumbles here and there...
All this time, your pompous ego had no idea….
I am the wolfbane to your vampiric existence.

Be My Fall

The end of summer is what I am celebrating,
That scorching heat, that endless sweating, be gone!
Come my rain, come my thunder, come my lightning,
Light my way, they will hear us roar and flood!

Random Thoughts

In 21st freaking century,
We are still dealing with
Toxic masculinity of
Cavemen, trying to
Mansplaining us.

May be we should
Just stuff them back
To the cavern
They climbed upon.

Do Not Even Get Me Started

They say, *''Choices are what truly ever matter,''*
As if we are given the right to choose on every aspect.
Please do tell hypocrite society,
What kind of a woman you think
Chooses to be raped / silenced / killed / beaten by
A man??????

Recycling

I have this fury deep inside me,
Coded and planted into my blood,
My vision goes all red,
Whenever I see toxic.
Some people should be locked up
Into biological hazard garbage bins.
Let them roth please.
We should sort them out.

God

I envision God as a judgemental narcissist,
Looking down from dreamy clouds,
Watching us like a TV freak show,
Sipping his ambrosia,
Laughing at us with angels/robots.

Evolving My Traumas

Wounds will heal,
Evolve into scars.
The traumas we have
Will be tucked in safely
Into the corners of our minds,
To grow and come back
For another day.

Sound Of Sisterhood

Silent and well-calculated steps,
We do not wanna scare our prey.
Guns loaded, all senses alert,
We go deeper and deeper
Into the woods.
We will hunt you down.

Rephrase

"I am love sick," I said,
He grinned, I rephrased for him,
"I am sick of the toxic love of yours."
He underestimates my words no more.
Mission accomplished.

Insert Sarcasm Here

All the kids are happy,
Look at their smiling faces!!!!
Nobody is all, all glitters and unicorn and rainbows!!!!
Oh my, oh my, what a freakin' positive dreamland!

Salute To Myself

I love myself,
I am strong,
I am a survivor,
I roar and laugh
As I slay
All the toxic ties.

Utopic

Stepped into a dream,
No women gets hurt or raped,
Let's stay in this dream.

Closure

Closing the doors behind you,
Never understood why you bothered
To leave them open,
As if it is possible for you
To turn back
After the bridge is burnt.

Telepathic

Funny, how you think
I do not know
What you have done.
I am always, always
Lurking
In the shadows
Of your mind.

Blind And Domesticated

You, thinking I will sit around,
Wait for you to be back,
Like any good house dog,
Blindly loyal, unconditional love,
Now, this is the best joke
I had heard in a while.

Tales

I am your medusa.
The hate you see in my eyes
Will turn your heart
Into a stone.

Slaying Game

You call me cold and cruel,
I think, you kinda have a point.
I can rip off my skin without flinching,
Not minding the pain, the blood
On my hands.
I cut open my own wounds,
I have a high tolerance for pain.

So now,
What makes you think of the tiny possibility
Of me to have any kind of mercy for you,
When my time comes?

Chin Up!

We fall,
We rise,
We laugh,
We cry.
Every single day,
We stand up and fight!

Falling Into FALL

"Finally some rain." I said.
The sky roared.
Washed my sins away.
I watched the gray sky in peace.
Clouds shooed the scorching sun away from my skin.
Heavens cried my tears,
I got to keep mine buried deep within.
Thunder sang me a love song.
Wind swept my heart breaks away.
Hey lightening,
Lead my way home,
Hey lightening,
Lit my cigarette.

Pumpkin Carving

All these words of mine
That fell so deaf on your ears
Are gonna be what
I carved into your consciousness.
I wish for you to know,
You will never see me fall.

Beast And Queen

Your control over me
Slips from your hands,
The way your mask
Slips from your face
When we are alone.
They see an educated man
Who loves me dearly.
I only see a beast in disguise.
A beast that is hungry
For the love
I will not give.
Poor, poor beast.

Demon In Disguise

I tucked my wings in,
You assumed and labeled
Me as a fallen angel.
Poor baby,
Speechless
Once he sees me,
In my full glory,
Black wings,
Steel skin.

Cradle Of A Mother

Cradle me to your chest, Mother Earth,
Today is another battle we had lost.
The hit I took in the name of love,
Is gonna be my death one of these days.
Cradle me Mother, cover me with earth.
Nobody else can keep me safe,
Give me space to rest and we create
Another day, another opportunity to face
The enemy in the name of love.

Ferrari And The Red Light

My life feels like
A sports car
Stuck in the loop of a red light.
I can go fast,
Society forced me to stop.

Mirror Talk

You try to break me over and over,
Claiming the light will get in.
I use my words to fill the cracks,
My hatred is a reflection
Of the poor man
You see
Every day
In the mirror.

Playing With God

Playing deaf, blind and mute,
Yet screaming on top your lungs
That you are the authority,
Like a toddler tantrum.
Do tell me God,
When we pray, does it make you laugh?
You heard it all so much, different languages,
Did it go straight to your head?
If you will play the ignoring game,
Let's play, I am all-in.

What Has The World Come To?

This world was your canvas,
You created blood, violence,
Murders, rapes….
Now you are pouting
Cos your painting
Looks like s*ht.

BonFire

Watch me burn these bridges,
You were too afraid to cross.
Girl, let's lit
A bonfire to celebrate.

GraveDigger

Traveled heart to heart
Until the last stop, you fear,
Who will bury you?

Long Lost, Never Found

Brain of scatter,
What's the matter?
Too thick, your batter?
Your meaningless chatter,
You take the hit, shatter,
Shatter, shatter, shatter….

I pick up your pieces,
Scattered ideas,
Biased speeches,
Carnival of memories,
Nowhere it reaches….

Reins Of A Puppet

"How do you cope with so much trauma and pain?"
Onlookers ask all the survivors.
My inner strength blooms from my scars,
Blood blooms blood-thirsty from my tears.
You gave trauma and pain,
I bloomed into a cruel, evil queen
You look upon, holding your reins.
Who's laughing now?

Zombie

When this shit show is over,
When you feel lonely and
Ask for my letters,
That is when this break-up
Will hit you the most.
Without my words,
You are just dull and dead.

Snub It Out

Society is the cigarettes
I snub on my own skin.
Always extinguished ,
Left its mark on the armor of my skin.

Past Tense

Walking past near you,
Providing no past will haunt me down.

I use simple past tense,
When I talk about you nowadays.

My Brutal Honesty

I had burnt so many bridges,
For which I am proud of.
They all tried to tame me down
Into a dull, mute puppet,
Make me eat their harsh words
Served as breakfast, lunch, dinner
And in-between snacks.
Called me names when I
Obviously did not listen,
I'll admit, sometimes, mannnn,
They got so freakin' creative.

In the age of 35,
Standing tall and strong,
I'll admit, there's no space,
There is no place
In my heart
Except for my kids.

Makes me wonder sometimes,
Do I really want to be loved?
Can I be really loved,
Without trying to be tamed?

You know,
Most of the days,
I do not even think about it.

But again sometimes,
It feels like an itch on my skin,
I want to rip it off with my bare hands
For some relief.

I guess even if I were
Handed a lover,
With the sarcastic, brutal, restless
Nature I have,
I would burn that one down
To the ashes too....

So there's that,
My freakin' truth,
How I feel like hypocrite
Writing all these poems down,
Well-knowing,
I am not made for that shit.

I Am Not Here To Please The World   Cathy BLUE

But again,
As the mere human being
I am, may be,
A slightly may be,
I will always chase after
What I can never have.
Cos now, my loyalty,
It does not belong to me anymore.

What belongs to me is to roar and protect,
An endless fury to stand against to the all forcings of
Society and take the hit, when needed,
'Cos we all know by now,
I have freakin' high pain tolerance.

Cut open, stitch back,
Cut open again, watch it bleed,
Clean the wound, stitch back,
To cut open, again, another day.

Beast&Me

You, after all these fights we had,
After all playing God to me,
Trying to make me submit to you
Makes my anger roar,
Ice blooms in my veins,
I don't hold back the beast anymore.

The Strength In My Bones

How naive of you to think,
I can be melted down,
Stuffed in a funky mold
To be reshaped as Society wants.
Try to melt me down,
Watch how my lava scorches your soul.
I'll always be what I have been,
A strong outsider to all onlookers.

What Humanity?

It is like watching a black&white TV,
Me switching on and off of my humanity.
Switch it on, bleed, cry and write,
Switch it off, when you are done.

Sugar-Coating

Trying to bait my heart out
With a promise of
A promise of heaven,
Makes me sigh in exasperation,
Do you think I am so dumb
That I can not even see
How you sugarcoat
A Piece of hell
In the disguise of a heaven?
Been there, done that,
Got demon lovers to play
In return.

Swallowed Fireworks

Down on your knees,
In front of me,
Begging for mercy,
Forgiveness as well,
Way too late.

The pleasure of being right,
All the time,
Being the strong one,
Having the upper hand
In this game of two,
Man, oh poor man,
I've never felt so alive.

Birth Of A Goddess

Your love is a myth,
I got burnt, scorched down
To my bones.
I picked up myself,
Filled golden inside my bones,
Gave birth to A Goddess.
Now you pray.

Wolf In Sheep Skin

A demon on human skin,
I deceive all the eyes
Who only sees a lovely face
In the crowd.
Here and there,
You see my quirks,
You feel the pull of
My magnetic energy.
You fall for the traps
I had set,
Do tell,
Who's your favorite demon today?

Self-Salvation

Standing in front of the mirror,
I gaze back and talk to myself,
What do I wait for?
What do I hope,
What do I hold on to?
Would not it be foolish
To hope for better days?
''Hush, hush,'' says the naive heart-
As if she has never take a hit
And bled to her death many times-
''We are waiting for better days,
They will come,'' in that
Effin irritating sing-song voice.
I hold my own gaze,
Pull the trigger to my heart,
I won't be fooled anymore.

Force Of Nature

Written in the clouds,
sudden lightening, my heart,
Furious and bright.

Thunder takes over,
Blissful silence of my thoughts,
I laugh when it roars.

Storm, unite my soul,
Make me powerful, mighty
A force of nature.

Dreams Of NeverLand

In the blink of an eye,
Time is running out.
I am levitating from my human shelf,
Cries of pain and absolute fear welcomes me,
"We were waiting for you," they whisper
Inside my head, ushering me inside.
There will be hell to pay for that....

Puppet Birth

Well-calculated, an amazing manipulator,
Mummy dearest,
Ripped all the remiges of my wings,
A punishment of still wearing her look,
Yet, unable to fly away, now...

Society Tunes

Fingers,
Squeezing life out of me,
Restless, cold-blood, callous,
Gleeful, cunning, clingy….
Can't even breathe...

White Lies

*''Don't stop, You're doing great, yeasss, that spot
there,''*
And all the other lies, we have to tell to man,
Whom can't find his way with a freakin' map in hand.

I Dare You

I blink back my tears,
Swallow down my tears,
This sick Society of heirs,
All the endless questionnaires,
Will not tackle us down
To their low level.

Toxic Love

Swirling around my body,
Wrapping yourself around my body,
Embracing every inch of my body,
Suffocating the life out of my body...

Misfit

They tried to break me apart,
Went straight for the heart.
Broken and bandaged,
Still beating,
Still pumping fury
To my mundane body.
Society,
I own you.

Breeze

I am unable to survive
Under this scorching sun,
Shining to blind,
Shining to desert my body.
Enough of this heat,
I need a cool breeze
To blow away the
Needles under my skin.

Fury Of The Demon

Run little human run,
I am gonna hunt you down,
Limb by limp,
I will tear you apart,
I will dismount all your bones
To make a new wall art on my wall.
The crimson of your blood
Splashed all over my white wall,
An abstract art of my like.
MMMMM,
I'm gonna hunt you down.
Your time is running out.

Embrace Your Inner Demon

That fury I was given,
The beast they all lamely tried to tame,
My inner dragon, my lover demon,
Roar for us, open your wings wide,
Hover over my heated skin.
You and I, side by side,
Will live forever,
Together.

Inner Strength

You can try to tame me,
Chain me down,
Cut off my tongue.
It is the devil in me
You should be afraid,
Unleashed, unlimited imagination,
Untamed, cruel, numb to the emotions.
Now, society dearest,
How fast can you run?

Sweeping The Dirt

I inherited the fury of the wind,
From the ancestors of mine,
Restless, strong, cold,
A non-stoppable force of nature.
All these walls you foolishly tried to erect
Will teach you what wind erosion means.
My fury, your contribution to it….
I will erose it all till your bones,
Sweep it all, under the rug.

Reasoning

All your childish tantrums
Depend on the fact that
I no more want to
Spend time with you.
You acknowledge your frustration,
I look down, sigh heavily,
Rejecting the mummy role
I am supposed to play
With a 40-year-old man.

Cat And Mouse

I breathe in, I breathe out,
Time stays still between my breathing,
Forms into a white smoke,
Hanging up in the air,
Between who I was yesteryear,
What I am now.
I blink, time slips inside my nostrils,
Poufff, it's all gone now!

Binge-Watching

These onlookers have zero self-respect,
Who can watch TV all day,
Without understanding what they even watch?
I speak fire, roar it out,
They want with a blank look on their face,
Zero brain cell in their skulls.

The Director

You talk about how proud you are
About what I achieve without you.
I watch you in silence,
Not gonna spend my precious words
On your trivial self-monolog
To play your supportive
To the meaningless onlookers.

Returning The Favor

The world tried to take me down
A couple of times,
Cut me open, left to bleed out,
I stitched myself back,
Wiped the gore from my bruised skin.
Took a deep breath, chin up,
This cycle of pain I have been given
Is only adding more to my strength
Restless determination
To return the favor.

Enemy Within

Shards of glass sprinkling down my spine,
These words we bury into a deep silence,
The things we play to ignore for ourselves,
Heart, stupid, silly naive heart,
You are my biggest enemy.

:)
Curse the light,
Blame the tools,
Get a scapegoat….
The fact of you
Being so incapable
Does not change now,
Does it?

Hush Little Prey

Hush little prey,
Be silent and pray,
Your demon will rip you apart,
Stitch you back insides out.

Hush little prey,
Time came to pay.
I am here to play,
Until you decay.

Hush little prey,
My authority, you obey.
Today is not the day,
You reek of sensual dismay.

Hush little prey,
Your demon will slay,
Your soul I will convey,
So many sins to pay.

I Am Not Here To Please The World   Cathy BLUE

Hush little prey,
We play human and demon today,
It'll be fun, I promise, I say,
Why don't you, a little longer, stay?

Hush little prey,
I see the way,
You I'll display,
You're my human clay.

Hush little prey,
Now, my time to play,
What a lovely broken clay,
Hip hip hooray!!!!!

And The Oscar Goes To

Glamor me,
Make me dazzle,
Make me look pretty
And divine,
With a million dollar smile,
Kill the Goddess inside me.

Nobody cares what you think,
What you feel,
What you laugh at,
What makes you cry,
What makes you bawl your eyes out.

They all want this big, fake smile,
You practice in front of the mirror,
All day long.
Smile and deflect the questions,
Play stupid and win,
Noone wants real answers.

They will cover you in gold,
Create a Goddess out of you,

I Am Not Here To Please The World   Cathy BLUE

Right after they kill
The Goddess in you.

Put on a lipstick,
Smile big and happy.
Put on a fur coat,
Warm the hollow of your soul.
Put on a black little dress,
Play your part, be a mute doll.

They'll die to be near you,
Grabby hands for every part of you,
All your clothes, books,
Furniture, hair, undies, even nails….

Sell your soul,
Noone cares about it anymore.
Sweetheart, it's your body,
They want, they lust,
They can't get enough!!!!!

Fake a smile, carry on.
Die a little inside, carry on.
Noone cares who you are, MOVE ON!

Wiping The Blood From My Knuckles

I came, i fought,
Some I lost,
Most I won!
I am proud of myself,
Never went down,
Without a good fight.

Self-Motivation

Drop the deadweight,
Unloose yourself.
Cut toxic ties,
Untangle your own mess.
Fly solo baby girl,
You need to go high,
All these stars are yours to take.

How Do You Like Your Coffee?

A Black coffee, please,
As black as my cold, dark soul,
Tastes sweet on my lips.

Spotlight

All these onlookers are talking behind my back,
Dahlin', it is soooo bright in the spotlight,
I can't see you, you look so small.
Dahlin', it is sooooooo loud up here,
All the applause and whistles,
I can't hear you really,
Sorry not sorry.

Come For Me

Hide under my bed
Come out every night to play
Who's the monster? Prey?

Devour me, eat me,
Rip out my cold, old black heart,
Feast on my warm blood.

Drip, drip, watch it pool
Shall we skinny dip? You, I?
Promise, it is fun!!!

Swim me laps, monster,
I'll take you for a wild ride,
I'll hunt you down. RUN!

Fall To Die

Earth shatters on us,
Diamonds fly, stab our eyes,
Now we are all blind.

I feel trees seek for
A piece to earth to hold on,
Nothing, paralyzed.

I hear the wolves howl,
Diamonds bleed in our ears,
We are all deaf, now.

I want to scream out,
To warn, words, no, I eat glass,
Muted we all are.

That is how earth falls,
Taking me, you, us down with
Look now, none survives.

Dance To Tempt

Can't run from my beat,
You'll dance for me, my sweet heat,
You'll sway to my beat.

One step at a time,
Come closer my little prey,
Dance into madness.

Oblivious world,
I am your damn world, touch, feel,
See, Hear, Taste me out.

I am your temptress,
Little fly on my cobweb,
Dance prey, sway, bleed, feed.

Dueling

One more or one less
Will it make any difference to me
If you punch me
Again in the heart?
I'll survive,
I'll armor up,
I'll hunt you down.
I'll haunt you down.

Extra-Ordinary

I am not your
Ordinary scapegoat,
You forgot to put a blindfold on me,
You forgot to cut off my tongue,
You forgot to tie me down to a wooden stake.

I see it all,
I hear it all,
I will say it all,
When the time comes.

Foreplay

Spread me wide open,
Tied up, all at your mercy,
Make me beg for all
You can give.
Scorch me, mark me,
Give it all,
Demonic pleasures,
My Incubus,
Tear me apart.

Panic Settling

I want to scream it out,
Words are clogged up my throat.
I want to break things,
Throw all the glassware to these white walls,
-You will have to clean that up.-
Deep breaths, this is my darkest night,
Cry a little, rock yourself, kiss your shoulder,
There is no light at sight.
Take a shot of Jager, feel it set you in fire,
Stop crying useless btch,
Take a deep damn breath.
Slow down, stop screaming at me,
Fcking loud brain!!!! Stop that bullshit!!
Stop it or I will shoot you in the head.

Kill To Live

Try to kick me all the more
When I am doubled down.
A few broken ribs,
Did you think
It will stop me?
Try to break me,
You make me
Darker, slyer, smarter, colder, cruel.
Still, I'll rise,
Watching the blood trickle down
From your head.

Questionnaire

You say i am a beautiful disaster,
Beautiful inside or outside?
Just a pretty face or that sharp tongue?
Is it real, what you see or just a reflection?

Eye To Eye With A Dragon

I looked at you in the eye,
Watching you roar flames
Over my steel armor.
You made me hot and seethering
Under my collar,
A little Scorched may be.

Silly little dragon,
I am The flame of my soul,
A little fire is nothing to me.
I had been to hell many times.
I hope, for your own sake,
You do not get to see me
Roar.

Blindfold

Keep adding trauma over trauma,
Lashing out whenever you are wrong,
Harsh words, belittling sessions for the onlookers....
Go on, carry on, I'm watching with a smirk on my face.
How I've changed you claim,
Stupid man, I only unfolded the blindfold.

The Digger

Try you might
To cover your lies,
Throw a fit
Over any doubts
I have/you gave.

That restless mind of mine
Will not stop digging
Into your conscious
Until all lies are
Revealed.

Folding Game

I like keeping things neat,
Like a damn pro,
I fold pain over heartbreaks
To maximize the space
In my closet,
To home
Many more to come.

Dirt Bags

They rubbed their dirty hands on me,
Wiped them clean and dry,
Threw me away when done,
Claiming I was the dirty one.
O'dear Society of hypocrites ….

Playing With My Favorite Demon

Peel my skin off,
Layer by layer.
Get me bare and naked,
I want to be a bad girl,
At your mercy.
Lower your head,
Let your horns graze and mark
My heated skin.

My body is yours to take,
Your tail, ohhhhh, I, I did not know
You could do that!!!!!
Yes now, I am aware,
Very aware, how close I am
To the peak.

Rip me wide open,
That's the only way
My demon will fit in,
I'll be a warm, snug hilt,
For your lengthy sword.

I Am Not Here To Please The World   Cathy BLUE

Move inside me,
Shift everything,
Rearrange all my insides,
Burn, mark, scorch all my inner walls,
Already crumbling down around you.

Oh my, do you feel it too?
I'm not sure where I start,
Where I end,
The pressure is too much.

Demon lover of mine,
Take me to your hell,
Lock me up in a cell,
Every damn night,
Torture and exorcise
My body and soul,
Well spent.

Changing Places

I sat on your throne,
Sipped your ambrosia,
An angel brought me pop-corn,
Many demons sat down beside my feet,
To watch the drama of life
Beneath our feet.

All the strings you put on humans
Got tangled only because
You did a half-hearted job,
Claim how almighty you are,
This drama goes very well with pop-corn.

Heart-breaks, disasters, violence, crimes,
Like a frakin' Titanic,
We watch the world
Sail headfirst into a big, freakin' iceberg.
We gasp when we are programmed to
Then stuff more pop-corn in our mouth.

I hear you begging for your life,
Dear God in human disguise,

I Am Not Here To Please The World   Cathy BLUE

I smile wide and do what you had always done to us:
Stuff more pop-corn into my damn mouth,
Take a big sip of ambrosia,
Clap, clap, clap!!!!!!!!

PLEASURES

P-lease me
L-ick my demon skin
E-ager to please me
A-im for lower,
S-lip into my darkness
U-nsure but determined,
R-ock my world,
E-lavate my soul.

CRAVIN'

Addicted to the fight I am in,
The thrill of having upper hand,
The knowledge of I am immortal-you are not,
Addicted to killing you every single day.

Spine Curls

S-talker demon on mine,
P-ausing pleasing himself,
I-nside he is dead, like the rest of us.
N-ot anymore he tries to hide that darkness,
E-asy how he claims my madness as his.

C-overs my soul with his darkness,
H-overs above my heart, in that gazing/pissing contest,
I- do not wanna let him down, I do not wanna lose too.
L-ies, sugarcoated on our tongue, his tongue is
L-icking all my sweet lies off of my human skin,
I-know we will never go back to what we were before,
N-ot that I care anymore, I want him inside so much,
G-rind my human soul, knead it into yours.

Beauty Within

Many scars I own,
Got nothing to hide from you,
What you see, real.

Never cover them,
You survived worst, a bit claws
On your fragile skin.

You ask me how to,
I am beautiful within
Don't need you agree.

Hangry Crocodiles In My Sea

Walk the plank of my heart,
Don't look down, don't be scared,
Just a bunch of very
Hangry crocodiles in my sea.
How far, can you swim?
You can survive life with 1 leg still,
Give them an offering for me.

Your lies, your useless words,
I don't care anymore!
Talk to the parrot, mate!
I see pretty well with 1 eye,
Crystal clear lies of the soul,
1 eye patch to cover the ugliness of the soul!

On and off, you speak still,
Take a step, leap of faith,
Only hangry crocodiles in my sea.

Survivors Of Toxic

Every toxic relation is
Cancer of your soul,
Cut yourself open,
Clean it out,
Before it roots
in too deep.

Enslaving Rage

This untamed rage
Growing inside my rib cage
Can't turn the damn page,
Not enough cleansing of a sage.

Myself, I have to disengage,
This rage, I can't change,
This rage,I tried to exchange
Now, too late to leave the stage.

My untamed, endless rage,
I wanna put you in a cage,
Lock away, turn the page,
Throw the key, leave the stage.

Man On The Mirror

I will not have you
Try to clean your hands
Out of the mess
You had caused,
Playing the three monkeys.

I will not give you a bed
To rest or sleep.
I will not give you
Anything except
A big mirror,
Reflecting
Your
Biggest
Self-guilt.

Roar Of the Lioness

-for Emily, I'll always love you, soul sister-

Roar my lovely,
You've been a lioness,
They tried to cage you,
Tie you down,
Tame you to a domestic-home cat
For so freakin' long!
Fugile attempts it remained,
Clipping your nails.
Roar my darling,
You are a lioness,
It's now our time to prey
On those
Who tried to hold us down
For so long!

Mirror, Mirror

Complain about the hate you see
In my eyes,
It is just you, looking in the mirror,
Judging your own reflection

You are resentful to me
Hate me for me to be
The first one to say
I do not love you anymore.

Daring You Out

In my life,
Never met a soul
Who didn't have
Any resentments for me,
Mostly for something
I had done,
Cos they did not have the guts
To admit they were wrong.
Sometimes ironically for
Something I had done
Cos they read me wrong.

You, saying me your resentment today,
Only makes me smile cos it is nothing new.
I guess i will always be a villain in every story
I have to take a part, nothing exciting for me,
I had been playing for too long,
I had mastered it, I got so many oscars.

One thing is funny though, you still
Assuming I have a heart, that you can hurt.
It was my weakest point, I pulled the trigger
Without a blink, kill the weak part to stay alive.

So, if you are still thinking you can hurt me,
I dare you to read this poem all over,
You will hear my power, my demons sneaking
In between my words,
So bring it on! I do not have a heart you can stab.

Are you afraid I will stab yours?
Bring it on, I dare you,
Pull the trigger, let's see who will die first
Underestimate me, I promise it will be fun.
Fight me, I will slay you alive,
You are gonna be absolutely nothing
But a feast for my demons.

Message Taken

I will not pick up a fight,
Not this time.
I read you out,
Chapter by chapter,
Page by page,
In between these sneaky lines.

You had given me so many things,
Most bad to be honest,
Yet the good, small things you gave me
Made me a better person,
Gave me so much love and hope,
Purpose to live.

I read you out, universe,
I let it go, it was beautiful,
It was not mine.

I am ready for the gift you have given me,
My fury, my restless energy,
I have a feeling, a very strong feeling,

I Am Not Here To Please The World   Cathy BLUE

This time, we will burn down
More than a few bridges.

I feel it, I taste it in the air,
I am ready,
Let the time stall
As much as it can.
We are ready.